Introduction

Today's quilters, sewers, and crafters have fallen in love with yo-yos all over again!! What is old is now brand new. Yo-yos are easy to make with all the wonderful fabrics recently on the market. They are convenient to carry with you as a "lap top" project, and are perfect for embellishments on ready-made garments or made-from-scratch clothing and accessories. And, Clover needlecraft offers the Quick Yo-yo Makers – simple tools that make yo-yos in several shapes and sizes and make them FAST, FUN, and PERFECT every time.

My mother and I have collaborated on this book to create some "wearable" ideas for you that are fashion forward yet incorporate a retro feeling so very popular in clothing and accessories today. We hope you enjoy and expand upon many of our ideas and have as much fun making your yo-yo projects as we did creating them for you.

Yo-yos of Yesteryear

The yo-yo quilt with its many interesting color patterns was a popular design from 1920 to 1940. The yo-yos were made from small circles of fabric gathered into flat-like pouches and then sewn together into quilts or pillow tops. The quilts were easy to make from these small circles of fabric, because women could carry them and work on them wherever they went. Many of these quilts were made from readily available feed sack fabrics, some of which are now being reproduced for the market today.

The name yo-yo is given to these small gathered fabric circles and comes from the Yo-Yo toy, which was also very popular at that time. (The toy has two disks with a looped string around a center axle.) A Filipino, Pedro Flores, introduced it to the United States and sold it to Donald Duncan who received a trademark in 1932 for the word Yo-Yo.

Today the yo-yo quilt is experiencing a revival using contemporary color palettes and designs.

Acknowledgements

A special thanks to my mother, Donna Martin, who created the majority of the projects in the title. Her creative talent, energy, and enthusiasm have contributed to the success of my business for over fifteen years. I am grateful to our production team- Secely Palmer, Dian Stanley, Kayte Price, Leslie Beck and Tracy Thompson.

This page features Yo-yo Pettifores—stuffed and embellished yo-yos in silks and velvets by Michele Muska. See Michele's purse and pincushion pictured in our Gallery, on page 47.

General Instructions

Yo-Yo: a novelty quilting technique in which circles of fabric are gathered into flat pouches and sewn together to make bedspreads or other items. The technique has roots in nineteenth-century handwork but became very popular in the twentieth century.

Embellishing is a favorite focus for the traditional circle shape, as well as, the new heart and flower shapes created from Clover's Quick Yo-yo Makers. The fabrics we have featured include cotton, silk, rayon and velvet in contemporary styling with simple yet sophisticated results. We have provided you instructions for making yo-yos with or without the Clover Quick Yo-yo Makers. We have also suggested our favorite tools and tips for using them.

Basic Supplies
Thread - Sewing to match your fabrics, heavy duty such as buttonhole, bead thread like nylon, invisible

Needles

Scissors

Tape Measure

Fabric Glue

Pins

EZ Quilting's Easy Circle Cutter and 18 mm rotary cutter (optional)

Clover's Quick Yo-yo Makers (optional)

How to Make Yo-yos using the Clover Quick Yo-yo Maker
This tool allows you to make evenly spaced stitches to create beautiful gathers, the perfect yo-yo every time!

❶ See the size chart for approximate diameter of the piece of fabric you will need for each shape. Place the fabric between the plate and disc. Snap together matching ridge lines and notches. Be sure to place fabric right side down in the plate (disc with the lip around the edge). The flat disc pops inside.

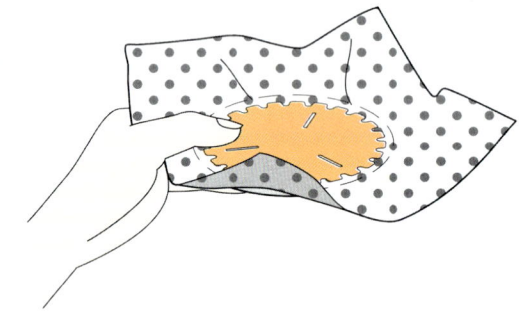

❷ Trim the fabric leaving approximately 1/8"-1/4".

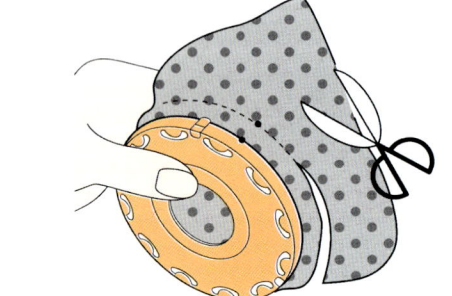

❸ Folding the seam allowance over the disc, stitch using a strong thread or doubled sewing thread through the fabric following the holes in the plate. Your last stitch should overlap your first.

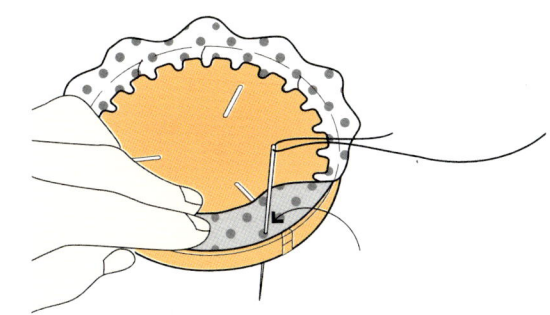

❹ Remove from the plate by pushing through the hole on the back of the plate. Gently pull the thread to gather fabric into a yo-yo. Flatten with the gathers centered on the top, pushing into shape as necessary. NOTE: The right side of the yo-yo is the gathered side. Insert the needle into the back side of the yo-yo through the center hole, take one stitch and knot the thread on the back side.

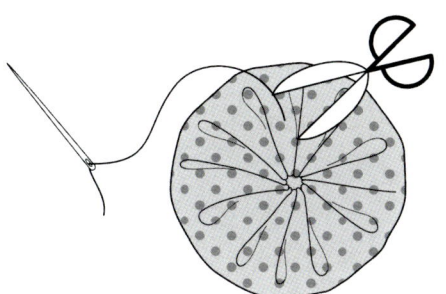

Cutting Chart

Cutting sizes for each Quick Yo-yo Maker

circles		shapes	
XS	2"	S flower	4 ½"
Small	3"	L flower	6"
Large	4"	S heart	3 ½"
XL	5 ½"	L heart	5"

Extra Large - Finished size 2½"

Large - Finished size 1¾"

Small - Finished size 1¼"

Extra Small - Finished size ¾"

Flower Shaped Small -
Finished size 1¼"

Flower Shaped Large -
Finished size 1¾"

Heart Shaped Small -
Finished size 1" x 1¼"

Flower Shaped Large -
Finished size 1½" x 1¾"

Instructions continued

How to Make Yo-yos without using the Clover Quick Yo-Yo Maker

❶ On the wrong side of the fabric, trace around the pattern piece using a water-soluble pen or pencil. Following your traced line, cut out the circle of fabric. (FYI: The cut fabric circles are twice the diameter of the desired finished yo-yo size plus a ½" for the seam allowance.)

❷ Finger press the raw edge of the circle a ¼" to the wrong side of the fabric, as you hand sew a running stitch close to the folded edge through both thicknesses. Use double thread (knotted) and make sure it is long enough to go around the full circumference of the circle with some to spare.

NOTE: Shorter stitches create a larger, more open center on your finished yo-yo. Longer stitches make a tighter finished yo-yo center. Medium to large stitches are recommended for the projects in this book.

❸ Once you have stitched around the entire perimeter of the fabric circle, your last stitch should overlap your first. Gently pull the thread to gather fabric into a yo-yo. Flatten with the gathers centered on the top, pushing into shape as necessary. NOTE: the right side of the yo-yo is the gathered side. Insert the needle into the back of the yo-yo through the center hole, take one stitch and knot the thread on the back side.

We recommend using the Clover Quick Yo-yo Maker Tool to make the heart and flower shaped yo-yos.

Make cutting quick and easy. Use EZ Quilting's EZ Circle Cutter and 18mm rotary cutter.

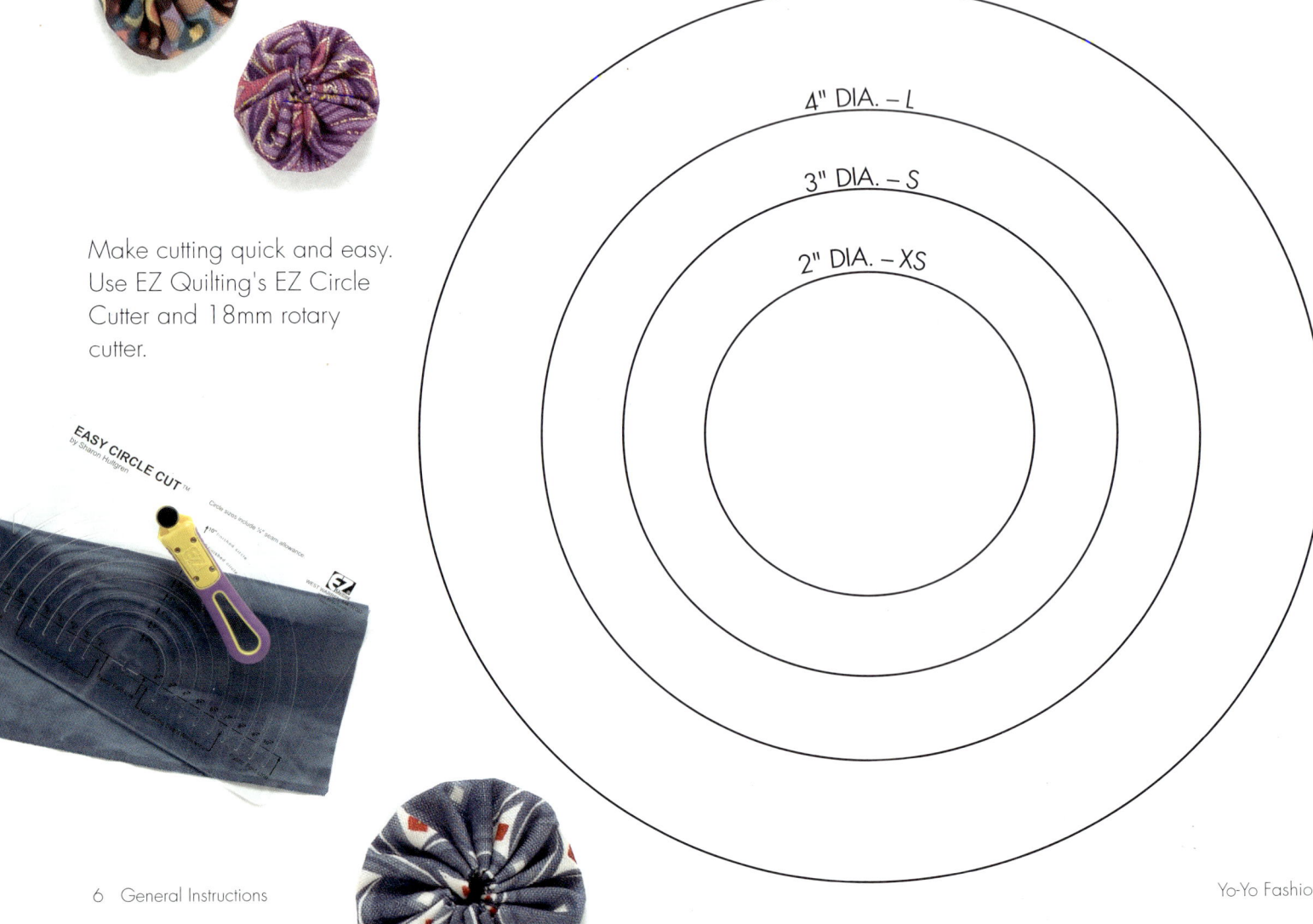

5½" DIA. – XL

4" DIA. – L

3" DIA. – S

2" DIA. – XS

General Directions for Stitching Yo-yos together

Lay yo-yos right sides together. (The right side of the yo-yo is the gathered side.) Stitch on the very edges of the adjacent yo-yo edges.

Embroidery stitches used for embellishments

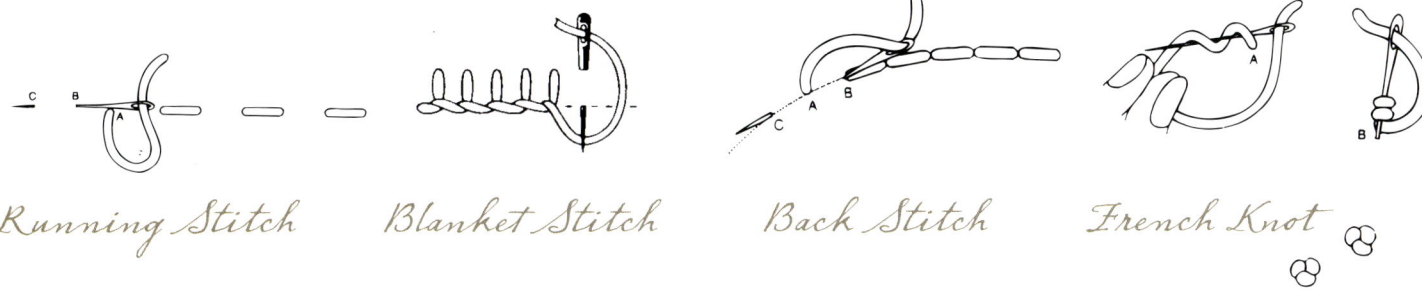

Running Stitch *Blanket Stitch* *Back Stitch* *French Knot*

How to Make Twisted Cord

Measure one strand of yarn approximately three times the desired length of your finished twisted cord. To determine the desired thickness of your twisted cord, add yarn strands to the first yarn piece that you cut and fold in half until desired thickness is reached. Unfold yarn pieces and tie each end to two pencils, per Illustration ❶. With two people each holding a pencil and facing each other, twist the pencils clockwise until the yarn is taut. When the yarn starts to kink in the center

have the first person hold both pencils while the other holds the center of the cord at the kink and lets the yarn twist onto itself, per Illustration ❷. Remove both ends from the pencils and knot together. Knot the opposite end to prevent unraveling. Our favorite tool for this process is Kreinik's Custom Corder. The hand-held tool twists together two or more strands of thread, ribbon or yarn to create cording for the belts, bags and jewelry.

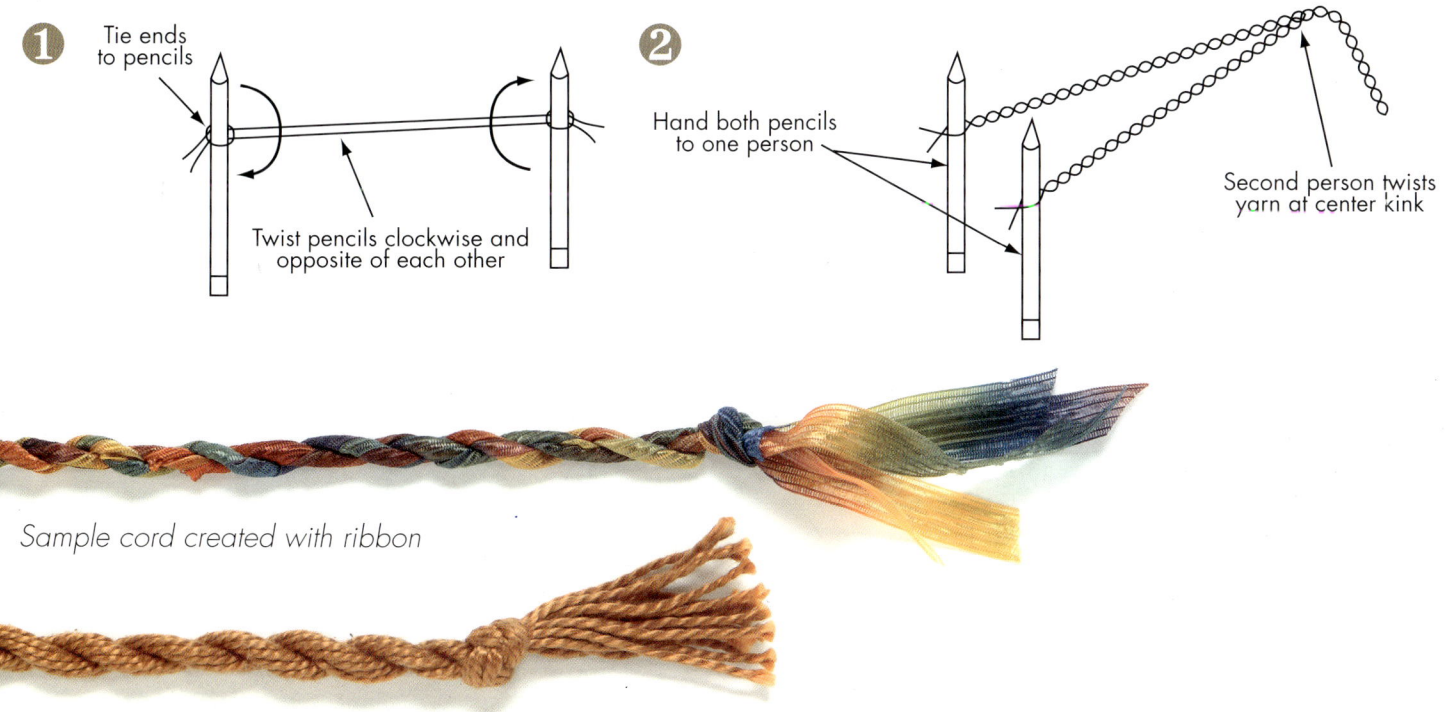

❶ Tie ends to pencils
Twist pencils clockwise and opposite of each other

❷ Hand both pencils to one person
Second person twists yarn at center kink

Sample cord created with ribbon

Sample cord created with perle cotton

Balloon Tee

Materials

One child's tee shirt

Five 4"x5" pieces of coordinating fabrics

Seven small pearl buttons

Perle cotton

Sewing thread

Children will love the dimensional aspect of this tee shirt design which combines yo-yos and hand stitching.

Instructions

❶ Make yo-yos: 1 large heart yo-yo, 2 small heart yo-yos, 2 small round yo-yos

❷ Arrange yo-yos on shirt to resemble balloon bouquet (refer to photo). Tack yo-yos to shirt leaving edges free.

❸ Sew buttons to centers of yo-yos.

❹ Cut five long lengths of perle cotton. Thread needle and knot one end only. To stitch the balloon strings, hand sew long running stitches from the base of each yo-yo. Refer to the photo for ideas. Bring the stitches together where the balloons would be tied together and then apart as if the balloon strings where free. Knot ends of each string on the back side of the tee shirt.

❺ Thread needle with a long length of perle cotton. Do not knot. Take the needle in one side at the location where the strings come together and out the opposite side from the back to the front at the point where the balloons would be tied together. Tie the ends in a bow and then knot bow to secure.

❻ To ruche the sleeves, mark sleeve center and measure up 3 inches from the bottom edge. Begin stitching downward using the perle cotton and a running stitch. Pull up the stitches to form ruching. Finish by sewing a button at the end to secure the stitching.

Creative Cuff Jeans

Materials

One Child's pair of jeans

Five 6"x 45"pieces of coordinating fabrics for yo-yos

One small pearl button

Key fob

Individualize a child's pair of jeans with yo-yos and hand embroidered embellishments. Drop a key chain yo-yo charm from the belt loop for good luck.

Instructions

❶ Turn pant leg cuffs up about 2". (This dimension may vary depending on child's size and height.)

❷ Make yo-yos using all the different fabrics: 11 large round, 10 small round, 1 small heart. (You may need more or less depending on size of jeans.)

❸ Stitch 5-large and 5-small yo-yos around turned up cuff alternating size and color.

❹ To make the key fob, stitch small heart yo-yo on top of a large yo-yo and attach to key fob.

Ideas

- Make for adult jeans
- Change the shape and color of the yo-yos and embellish with beads, rhinestones or buttons
- Use a yo-yo belt to carry out the yo-yo theme

Embellish a sweater to match your jeans. Add a single heart to a tee-shirt or sweater. (See Have a Heart Sweater, page 12.) A running stitch accent in perle cotton around the collar and down the front completes the design.

Young at Heart Belt

Materials

Variety of small print cotton fabric scraps, approximately 3" x 6"

Seventeen 3/8" diameter pearl buttons

6 yards of coordinating perle cotton for twisted cord ties

Ideas

- Use colors to match an outfit
- Make an adult size by increasing the number of yo-yos and/or increasing the size of the yo-yos
- Substitute beads for the buttons
- Change the sizes and shapes of the yo-yos. Try flower shaped yo-yos

Hearts and circles combine with buttons to make a charming little belt for a favorite pair of jeans or use to gather the waist of a long sweater. Child's belt is approximately 24" long without ties.

Instructions

❶ Make yo-yos: 8 small round, 2 small heart, 2 large round, 5 large heart

❷ Sew buttons to the center of each yo-yo.

❸ Lay yo-yos in a line until you achieve a pattern of coloration and size to your liking.

❹ Stitch yo-yos together by taking 4-5 small stitches on the edges of the two adjacent yo-yos. Repeat until all 17 yo-yos are stitched together in a row.

❺ Make two twisted cord ties, finished length approximately 7½" long. Refer to the General Directions for how to make the twisted cord ties. Knot both ends, leaving a little fringe on one end of each cord. Tack one cord to the back of the last yo-yo leaving the fringe end out. Repeat for the opposite end.

❻ Tie at the waist.

Have a Heart Sweater

Simplicity, just three hearts and a running stitch adorn this child's sweater to make it "Sweet and Simple".

Instructions

❶ Make 3 small heart yo-yos.

❷ Tack the yo-yos securely to the sweater on one side, vertically as shown in the photograph. Leave the edges of the yo-yos free.

❸ Sew buttons to the centers of the yo-yos.

❹ Stitch next to ribbing around neckline and down the front placket of the cardigan with ¼" running stitches. Repeat the running stitches on the ribbing at the cuffs of the sleeves.

Materials

Child's white cardigan sweater

Three scraps of printed red cotton fabric for yo-yos

Three pearl buttons

Red perle cotton

Ideas

• Use tiny ribbon or fancy yarn in place of the perle cotton
• Double the perle cotton to make a bigger statement
• Use a single large heart with button
• Use flower yo-yos instead of hearts

Fancy Flower Jeans

Materials

One 4" x 10" piece of green fabric for the leaves

Eight 4½" x 9" rectangles of cotton fabric in various colors for yo-yos

1½ yards of ½" wide flat black lace or medium rick rack

Black perle cotton

Sewing thread

Ideas

- Great for adult jeans
- Use around the neckline of a sweatshirt
- Group flowers and leaves together and embellish a tee shirt with a bouquet of yo-yo flowers

Decorate a pair of adult or child's jeans with a string of flower yo-yos, finish the top and bottom with a leaf. Trim bottom of legs and belt loops with black lace or rick-rack. This yo-yo embellishment was a vintage piece originally used as a curtain tie back. It was "reinvented" to embellish these children's jeans.

Instructions

❶ Stitch black lace or rick-rack to lower edge of jean legs and on to belt loops, see photograph.

❷ Cut four leaves from green fabric using the pattern below.

❸ Fold and press edges of leaves to the wrong side a ¼". Clip curves as necessary to create a smooth rounded edge. Blanket stitch around edge with perle cotton. Back stitch veins on leaves. See general instructions for embroidery stitches.

❹ For the flowers, make 16 large yo-yos, two from each fabric color. Do not pull the center tight. Leave a center opening of approximately ½". Take the needle through to the back side and knot. You may need more or less flowers depending on the length of your jeans

❺ Using black perle cotton, stitch five French Knots in the center opening of each yo-yo per the illustration below.

❻ Tack one leaf at the hem on the side seam, then follow with flowers up the side seam and finish with a leaf at the top front pocket edge. Repeat for the opposite leg.

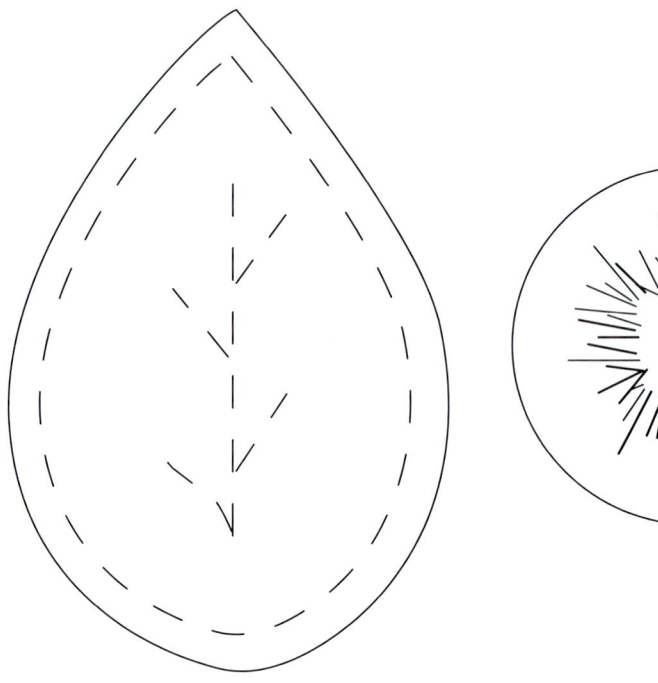

Collared Cardigan

Dress up a sweater with a yo-yo collar and embellish it with buttons.

Materials

Child's red cardigan sweater

Three ¼ yard pieces of coordinating red printed fabrics for yo-yos

Nine or more ½" diameter red buttons

Three 5/8" diameter dark red buttons

Optional: API Basting Glue

Instructions

❶ Make 23 small yo-yos using all the coordinating fabrics

❷ Arrange yo-yos to form a collar shape around the neck of the sweater. Refer to the photograph at right for placement.

❸ Stitch in place and embellish centers of some of the yo-yos with assorted buttons. TIP: Use API Basting Glue to hold yo-yos in place while you stitch them down.

❹ Add smaller red buttons to existing sweater buttons to create a stacked button look.

Ideas

• Use this on an adult sweater by increasing the number of yo-yos
• Add more buttons, beads or rhinestones to the center of the yo-yos
• Use contrasting, matching or a two-color combination of yo-yos and buttons

As a collared cardigan option, this accent incorporates two alternating sizes of yo-yos in two fabrics, with buttons between and in the center of the yo-yos.

Simple Scarf

Materials

Six ½ yard pieces of plain and printed silk or rayon blend fabrics in various shades of red, hot pink, and orange

Ideas

- Use a larger yo-yo maker which would be easier and take fewer yo-yos giving your scarf a totally different look
- Customize your color combination. Try brights, pastels and black and white
- Change the fabrics. Use cotton, batiks, satin or charm packs
- Adjust the size to make a belt or trim for a jacket or vest

Accessorize is the key word in fashion and this little scarf is perfect, especially in red to brighten your favorite black outfit. Approximate size is 3¾" wide x 63" long.

Instructions

❶ Make 150 small yo-yos using the various shades of fabric.

❷ Assemble rows of three yo-yos by stitching each yo-yo on its edge to the adjacent yo-yo using 5-6 small stitches. Don't overlap the edges. Mix and match yo-yos as you like. Make 50 sets of three yo-yos each.

❸ Layout 5-6 sets of 3 yo-yos and rearrange them until you are satisfied with the look. Stitch each row to the next by stitching each yo-yo on the edge to the corresponding yo-yo in the next row. Take 5-6 stitches to secure. Do not overlap.

❹ Repeat Step 3 until all yo-yo rows are assembled into 5-6 row sets. Sew these sets together as you did in Step 3 until all sets are sewn together and scarf is finished.

Reversible Neck Wraps

Materials

½ yard of overdyed velvet, Minkee™, or velour in overdyed jewel tones

One 5" x 45" piece of green silk

Three 3½" x 45" pieces of jewel tone silk

80 – 2mm beads

Optional: 8 yards of perle cotton to make twisted cord, finished length 12"

Ideas

- Use cotton fabrics for a casual look
- Make it very long and trim your Christmas tree

Wrap it around your neck or waist; trim a sweater neckline; or run it down a jacket front. A lovely length of yo-yos to play with and it is quite fancy. Finished size is approximately 40" long.

Instructions

❶ Make yo-yos: 10 extra large of velvet, 9 large of green silk, 10 small of jewel-tone silk

❷ Stitch the small yo-yos on top of the extra large yo-yos. Stitch 3 beads in the center of the front and back of the extra large yo-yos.

❸ Stitch 1 bead in the center on front and back of the each large yo-yo.

❹ Stitch the beaded yo-yos together beginning with and ending with an extra large velvet yo-yo. Alternate velvet and green silk yo-yos until all 19 yo-yos are stitched together side to side.

❺ If you are using this for a belt, make two 12" long finished twisted cord ties using 4 lengths of 36" perle cotton for each tie. Refer to the General Instructions on how to make twisted cord ties.

Silk Satchel

Materials

½ yard green silk for purse body, silk from Libas LTD., color #053

½ yard gold silk for purse lining, silk from Libas LTD., color #144

10 silk fat quarters (18"x 22" pre-cut fabric) in colors to coordinate with purse body. Libas LTD. colors: Pink #154, Light Red #220, Dark Red #074, Dark Brown #037, Light Brown #030, Gold #144, Dark Gold #114, Light Green #227, Dark Turquoise #024, and Light Turquoise #041

¼ yard felt (interfacing)

90 - 2 mm beads in coordinating colors

12 yards of variegated silk ribbon yarn (draw-string handle)

Optional: Clover Easy Turn Tool

Ideas

- Make the bag from denim and use feed sack reproduction fabrics for the yo-yos and embellish with small vintage buttons
- A combination of batiks would be fabulous made up in this purse as well as any number of fabric collections

Create this vintage-like drawstring purse from silk. Embellished with yo-yos and beads, it is fabulous for a night out.

Cutting Instructions

Exterior Purse body: (Green Silk)
    Two upper purse body sections using pattern piece on page 44
    Two 5" x 14" for lower purse body section
    5"x 7" oval for bottom exterior of purse
Interior Purse lining: (Gold SIlk)
    Two upper purse lining sections using pattern piece on page 44
    Two 5" x 14" for lower purse lining section
    5"x 7" oval for bottom lining of purse using pattern piece on page 44
Felt Interfacing:
    Two 5" x 14" lower purse section
    Two 5" x 7" ovals for purse bottom using pattern piece on page 44
Yo-yos:
    50 - 5½" diameter circles in the 10 colors of silk for extra-large yo-yos (cut 5 from each color, 3 will not be used)

Instructions

❶ Make 50 extra large yo-yos from the 5½" diameter fabric circles. Set aside.

❷ Zigzag or serge around all remaining silk pattern pieces to help keep fabric from fraying.

❸ With the right sides together and using a 3/8" seam allowance, stitch the two upper bag exterior body pieces together along the side seams making sure to leave an opening in both side seams as marked on the pattern piece for the draw string casing. Repeat for two upper bag interior lining pieces.

❹ With right sides together and using a 3/8" seam allowance, stitch the upper purse exterior section and the upper interior lining section together along the scalloped edge. CAREFULLY trim and clip curves of scallops and between scallops to seam allowance making sure not to clip seam open. Turn and press scalloped edge.

❺ Stitch a basting stitch along lower edge of upper purse section, to hold lining and purse exterior in place for later easing.

❻ To form drawstring casing along the top of the purse below scallops, topstitch two parallel rows, per stitch lines on the pattern piece. Set aside.

❼ Baste the two oval felt interfacing pieces to the wrong side of the exterior purse bottom piece.

❽ Baste the two lower felt interfacing pieces to the two lower exterior purse pieces on the wrong side.

continued on page 24

Silk Satchel, continued

❾ With right sides together and using a 3/8" seam allowance, stitch the side seams of the two lower exterior purse pieces. (The felt interfacing is attached to each piece.) Trim and press seams open.

❿ With right sides together and using a running stitch, sew the lower exterior purse section to the purse bottom exterior piece with a 3/8" seam allowance. Press seam towards purse bottom, trim and clip curves.

⓫ With right sides together, stitch the upper purse section (which has been lined already) to the lower purse section, matching side seams and easing seams if necessary. Trim and press seams down toward purse bottom. Turn wrong side out (lining side out). Set aside.

⓬ With right sides together, stitch the side seams of the two lining pieces together. This makes the lower lining. Stitch a running stitch around the bottom for gathering and easing.

⓭ With right sides together, stitch the lower lining section to the purse bottom lining piece, ease edges, leaving a 4" opening along the purse lining bottom seam for turning later.

⓮ With right sides together, slip the bottom lining section over the top of the upper purse section, matching the raw edges of the upper and lower lining sections. Stitch with a 3/8" seam allowance. Ease if necessary. Turn to right side through opening left in lining bottom, but do not close this opening until the yo-yos have been stitched in place.

⓯ Drawstring handle: Make drawstring by measuring three lengths of silk ribbon each 72" long and make a twisted cord (refer to General Instructions). Final cord should measure 24 inches. Make a second cord for other drawstring handle. Thread cord through drawstring opening on side seam of upper purse using the Clover Easy Turn or a large safety pin. Begin on one side and thread twisted cord completely around the purse and come out of the opening you started from. Repeat using second twisted cord, only start at the opposite side opening. Bring ends together and determine length you want the finished cords. These become your shoulder straps as well as your purse closures. Tie cords together in a knot.

⓰ Yo-yo embellishment: Begin pinning and stitching yo-yos on the seam where the upper and lower purse meet, be sure to cover the seam. Fourteen yo-yos should be evenly spaced and slightly overlapping side to side in the first row. Stitch a bead in the center of each yo-yo and in the spaces between the yo-yos. As you stitch the bead in place also catch the edges of the surrounding yo-yos to help stabilize. Place fourteen yo-yos in the next row down, again overlapping upper row and side to side, refer to photo. The third row curves over the bottom edge seam and uses twelve yo-yos. These must be sewn more securely because of the curving. The purse base is covered with seven yo-yos. Hand stitch yo-yos in place, sewing in the center of the yo-yo and side to side. DO THE HAND STITCHING OF THE YO-YOs AND BEADS THROUGH THE OPENING IN THE LINING. You can stitch the beads at this point or go back and stitch them on later after all the yo-yos have been stitched in place. After all the yo-yos are secured and the beading is completed, slip stitch lining opening closed.

Silk Sunflower

Instructions

❶ Make 3 extra small reddish-orange yo-yos and 1 extra large dark red silk yo-yo. Set aside.

❷ Fold orange silk in half lengthwise forming a strip 2" x 12". Stitch a running stitch 3/8" from bottom aligned raw edges, leaving long tails on thread. At 5/8" wide intervals, cut 1 ¼" from folded edge towards the raw edge, leaving ¾" uncut along the raw edges. See illustration, page 45.

❸ Pull thread and gather tightly forming a 4" circle of folded fringed silk.

❹ Stitch the felt circle to the back of the gathered circle.

❺ Pin and stitch the extra large yo-yo on top of the gathered circle.

❻ Stitch 3 beads to the center of each of the three extra small yo-yos. Stitch these yo-yos to the top of the one extra large yo-yo. Refer to photograph.

❼ Attach the pin back to the felt.

Materials

One 4" x 12" piece of orange silk*

One 6" x 6" piece of dark red silk* for extra large yo-yo

Three 3" x 3" scraps of reddish-orange silk* for extra small yo-yos

Nine 2mm beads

One 1¾" circle of coordinating felt for backing

One 1" pin back

*Sample used Libas silk duponi

Silk Chrysanthemum

Materials

One 6" x 18" piece of medium blue silk*

One 6" x 18" piece of light blue silk*

One 5/8" diameter button

One 3/4" circle of coordinating felt for backing

One 1" pin back

*Sample used Libas silk duponi

Instructions

❶ Make 1 small light blue yo-yo and 1 extra large medium blue yo-yo.

❷ Cut 1 - 2" x 12" strip of light blue silk
Cut 1 – 2½" x 12" strip of medium blue silk

❸ Cut each of the strips at 5/8" wide intervals leaving ¾" between bottom cut and fabric edge. See illustration, page 45.

❹ Lay the light blue strip on top of the medium blue strip with the uncut bottom edges together. Sew a running stitch 3/8" from bottom edge. Pull together tightly forming a 4 - 4½" circle. Stitch to secure.

❺ Stitch the felt circle to the back of the gathered circle.

❻ Stitch the extra large yo-yo in the center and on top of the gathered circle. Stitch the small yo-yo on top of the extra large yo-yo.

❼ Embellish the top of the small yo-yo with a 5/8" button.

❽ Attach the pin back to the felt.

❾ Pull the threads from the cut ends of the strips to form a fine fringe. Continue to pull the threads until the fringe is approximately ½" long.

All Seasons Sandal

Completely cover your flip flops with yo-yos and a button between your toes. You will be flipping and flopping in style.

Instructions

❶ Make 24 small yo-yos, six from each of the 4 coordinating fabrics

❷ Stitch yo-yos onto flip flop strap by stitching around the back of the strap and onto either side of the back of each yo-yo.

❸ Stitch six small yo-yos on each strap overlapping each one slightly.

❹ Stitch the thirteenth yo-yo to the toe strap (refer to photo for placement).

❺ Stitch a 7/8" diameter button in the center of the thirteenth yo-yo.

❻ Repeat for other flip flop.

Materials

One pair of plain black flip flops

Four 3" x 18" strips of fabric in coordinating cottons or silks for small yo-yos in jewel tone colors

Two 7/8" diameter buttons

Heavy-duty thread to match fabrics

Summer Fun! Try bright colors for our child's version.

Slip on Sandals

Materials

One pair of fabric slip-on sandals

Three 3" x 6" pieces of coordinating cotton fabrics

Two ½" diameter coordinating buttons

Yo-yo's can embellish many styles of shoes and this is just an example of an inexpensive fabric slip-on sandal that looks so cute with a yo-yo and button embellishment.

Instructions

❶ Make 6 small yo-yos, 3 for each sandal.

❷ Arrange the yo-yos in a horizontal line across the toe of the fabric sandal.

❸ Sew yo-yos in place across the top of the sandal.

❹ Embellish the yo-yos by sewing buttons to the centers. Repeat for second sandal.

Flowered Flip Flops

Coordinate your flip flops with your favorite outfit or just make some fun and flashy ones for you or a friend.

Instructions

❶ Cut two 2" X 22" bias strips from the printed orange fabric.

❷ Using one bias strip, wrap the strap of one of the flip flops. Beginning on the inside portion of the strap, fold one end of fabric under and wrap the strip over the folded end. Stitch in-place. Continue wrapping down the strap and over the top of the toe divider to the opposite side of the strap, using the entire length of the bias strip. Fold the opposite end under and stitch in place.

❸ Make 2 large flower yo-yos from the purple fabric and 2 small flower yo-yos from the orange fabric.

❹ Stitch the yo-yos together with the smaller yo-yo on top; arrange the yo-yos so the petals alternate.

❺ Finish by stitching a bead to the center of the flower and stitching the completed flower to the center of the flip flop above the toe divider. Repeat for the other flip flop.

Materials

One pair of flip flops

½ yard printed orange cotton fabric

One 6" x 12" piece of printed purple cotton fabric

Two 7mm purple beads

Beaded Belt

Materials

40" length of 7/8" wide brown velvet ribbon

Six 3" x 18" strips of coordinating fabrics in cotton or silk

36 - 2-mm beads

1 yard of 2½" wide bead-drop trim on a silk ribbon from Expo International

12 yards of perle cotton for twisted cord ties

Note: Materials may need to be adjusted based on your individual measurements.

Dress up a simple dress or skirt with an elegant bead and yo-yo belt. Finished adult length is approximately 36" long plus ties.

Instructions

❶ Stitch bead-drop trim to the edge, on the back side of the velvet ribbon beginning and finishing 1½" from either end.

❷ Make twist cords using 4 strands of 54" long wool yarn or perle cotton. Finished length of each tie is 18". Refer to the General Instructions for how to make the twisted cord ties.

❸ Slightly untwist the folded end of one twisted cord, opening enough to slip 1½" of the velvet ribbon through the loop. Fold the end of the velvet ribbon to the wrong side ½" and stitch the folded edge to the back of the ribbon, encasing the twisted tie. This secures the ties to the end of the belt. Repeat this process at the opposite end of the belt.

❹ Make 36-small yo-yos from the six coordinating fabrics. Six from each color.

❺ Arrange the yo-yos on the belt overlapping each one slightly. When satisfied with the arrangement, pin in place, stitch and embellish the center of each yo-yo with a single bead.

Eclectic Ensemble

Fabric and beads combine to make some interesting and very fashionable jewelry.

Instructions

Necklace

❶ Measure neck, being sure the length is comfortable for a choker-type neck lace and add 2". Cut velvet ribbon to the measured length. Fold both ends ¾" to the wrong side and stitch to secure. Stitch hook and eye in place on folded ends.

❷ Make 3 small yo-yos from each coordinating fabric. Stitch yo-yos together with the center yo-yo slightly lower and the other two behind and on either side of the center yo-yo. Refer to the photograph.

❸ Gather the beaded trim and stitch to the center of the middle yo-yo.

❹ Stitch the assorted beads to the centers of the yo-yo's and on top of the beaded trim
TIP: Additional beads could be sewn on the velvet choker for a fancier look

Bracelet

❶ Measure wrist, be sure the length is comfortable and add 2". Cut velvet ribbon to the measured length. Fold both ends ¾" to the wrong side and stitch to secure. Stitch hook and eye in place on folded ends.

❷ Make 6 small yo-yos from each coordinating fabric and embellish centers with 3 beads each.

❸ Stitch beaded trim to back edge of the velvet ribbon and evenly space yo-yos on right side of ribbon and stitch in place.

Necklace Materials

½ yard of 7/8" wide brown velvet ribbon

Three 3" squares of coordinating silk or cotton fabric for yo-yos

2" of 2½" wide bead-drop trim on a silk ribbon from Expo International

One 1¼" fabric-covered hook and eye

18 – 2mm assorted beads

Bracelet Materials

9" piece of 7/8" wide brown velvet ribbon

Six 3" squares of coordinating silk or cotton fabric

7" of 2½" wide bead-drop trim on a silk ribbon from Expo International

One 1¼" fabric covered hook and eye

18 – 2mm assorted beads

Spaghetti Strap Tee

Materials

One purchased spaghetti strap tee

Coordinating cotton fabric scraps, fabric charm pack, or fat quarters (18" x 22" pre-cut fabric) matching spaghetti strap tee

Ideas

• Change the fabric to silk or satin
• Change the contrast of the yo-yos and the tee shirt
• Use a different shape of neckline
• Add buttons or beads to the center of the yo-yos

Make today's most popular under-garment fabulous with yo-yos up and over the shoulders as well as across the front.

Instructions

❶ Make enough small yo-yos to cover the shoulder straps and front neckline of tee shirt. The example used 30 small yo-yos.

❷ Make 1 large yo-yo and 1 extra small yo-yo.

❸ Mark the center of the neckline with a pin. Tack the large yo-yo in place in several places, but leave the edges free.

❹ Attach the small yo-yos around the neckline and on the shoulder straps. The yo-yos should overlap slightly and be stitched to each other as well as the strap.

❺ Stitch an extra small yo-yo to the center of the front large yo-yo.

Sweater Set

Materials

One purchased sweater set

One 4" x 35" piece of coordinating cotton or silk fabric

Six ¾" diameter buttons

Twelve 4mm round beads

Ideas

- Add beads or small buttons to the center of the yo-yos
- Use buttons with different shapes
- Use vintage buttons
- Use shaped yo-yos (heart or flower)
- Use charms instead of beads

Not only are yo-yos reminiscent of years gone by but the "sweater set" as well. Embellish the sweaters with a similar shade of yo-yos, beads and buttons and bring them full circle to be very fashionable today.

Instructions

❶ Make 8 small yo-yos

❷ To decorate the sweater, follow the illustration below.
O = yo-yo X = button • = bead

❸ Sew yo-yos, buttons and beads to the sweater. Tack the yo-yos in several places but leave the edges free.

❹ To decorate the sweater shell, find the center point of the neckline and tack one yo-yo in several places leaving the edges free. Sew a bead on each side of yo-yo approximately ¼" from edge of center yo-yo.

Savvy Shrug

Materials

2½ - 3 yards of coordinating cotton fabrics OR 10 to 12 fat quarters (18" x 22" pre-cut fabric) for yo-yos

Optional: Buttonhole thread

Ideas

- Change the fabric to silk or satin
- Add buttons or beads to the center of the yo-yos at the neckline

Please refer to page 46 for pattern and placement diagrams.

This stylish shrug was made from part of an antique quilt that has been recycled into a fashionable shrug. The directions are to make your own yo-yos and will approximate the size of the original yo-yos. This is not an exact fitting style but rather a loose shrug which can be readjusted quite easily.

Instructions

❶ Make a tissue or muslin pattern using the diagram on page 46 and size chart below to determine your size. This will help you to determine the correct number and placement of yo-yos.

❷ Make the quantity and specified size of yo-yos based on the garment size determined in Step 1:
Size extra small/small   156 large yo-yos
Size medium   200 large yo-yos
Size large/extra-large   250 large yo-yos

❸ Lay out yo-yos on pattern piece made in Step 1 according to graphic pattern on page 46. Stitch yo-yos securely at edges, both vertically and horizontally.

❹ With wrong sides together, fold down upper row of yo-yos around neckline and stitch in place. This helps add stability to the neckline which frames the face.

Note: If arm holes are too tight, fold yo-yos around these openings in half and stitch or eliminate some of the yo-yos. If the shrug is too tight across the back, add another row of yo-yos down the middle of the back.

Optional: Use buttonhole thread and stitch a running stitch around the arm hole to prevent stretching.

Size chart	Extra-small Small	Medium	Large Extra-large
A	36¾	42	47¼
B	12¼	14	15¾
C	5¼	7	8¾
D	3½	3½	3½
E	7	8¾	10½
F	5¼	5¼	5¼
G	1¾	1¾	1¾
H	15¾	17½	19¼

Coveted Collar

Materials

Several cotton fat quarters to make 54-large yo-yos (one fat quarter will make approximately 20-large yo-yos).

24 assorted ¾" and ⅝" diameter pearl buttons

Optional: 50" of United Notions shell trim #2109-15
This was used on the example.

This oversized collar was made from an antique yo-yo pillow top. Consequently, the yo-yo size and construction will be a little different when you make your own. One size fits most.

Instructions

❶ Make 54 large yo-yos.

❷ Cut a 5" diameter circle from paper and lay 12 yo-yos edge to edge around the outside edge of this circle paper pattern piece. Stitch all 12 yo-yo's together, leaving circle open. This frames the neckline edge.

❸ Lay the second row of 18 yo-yos adjacent to and between the yo-yos of the first row. Stitch in place at their edges.

❹ Lay a third row of 24 yo-yos adjacent to and between the yo-yos of the second row. Stitch in place at their edges.

❺ Randomly stitch the 24-buttons on top of the yo-yos.

Optional: Stitch behind the third row of 24 yo-yos the shell button trim around the lower edge and down the center fronts of the yo-yo collar.

Tone on Tone Jacket & Tee

Materials

Three 6" x 18" pieces of coordinating cotton fabrics in beige, cream, and brown (for yo-yos)

One small lace appliqué, approximately 3" x 3"

Three large lace appliqués, approximately 6" x 3"

Seventeen small pearl buttons in a variety of shapes and sizes

Three ¾" diameter pearl buttons

Two 1½" diameter pearl buttons

Rit Dye™, sample used: brown and green or Tsuniko Inks

Optional: Fabric Glue to stabilize design on garment before sewing

Ideas

- Create an elegant jacket with rhinestones and jewel buttons, and silk yo-yos
- Add decorative stitching down the front placket
- Embellish the collar

Take a ready made jacket and give it a little pizzazz with over-dyed lace and yo-yos in three sizes, as well as a variety of different shaped pearl buttons.

Instructions for Jacket

1. Make yo-yos from the coordinating fabrics, 2 extra small, 9 small and 2 large

2. The sample uses lace painted with a diluted solution of dye. Use colors to coordinate with your jacket color and yo-yo fabrics. An alternative would be to purchase lace already dyed.

3. Layout the lace appliqués on the front and back of the jacket referring to the photograph for placement. Combine two appliqués to form one large appliqué for the left front that extends over the shoulder and onto the back side. This combined appliqué piece will now measure approximately 9" long. Pin and stitch in place by hand. Repeat for other lace embellishments.

4. Embellish the lace appliqués with yo-yos and buttons referring to the photographs.

Instructions for Coordinating Tee

1. Make yo-yos from the coordinating fabrics: 2 small, and 1 large

2. Embellish the matching tee with yo-yos. Add buttons to the center. Refer to the photograph for placement.

Fabric Collage Jacket

Take the denim jacket from the back of your closet and make it uniquely yours. This fast and easy way to embellish with fabric yo-yos, buttons, stitching and lace is sure to bring you rave reviews.

Materials

¼ yard of floral fabric to coordinate with your jacket for fan shaped embellishments (fan pattern pieces located in the pattern section)

Coordinating fabric scraps to match floral fabric for yo-yos

Perle Cotton for decorative stitching, color: cream

One 1" diameter button

One ¾" diameter button

One round sew-on pearl

Three lace appliqués, approximately 2½" x 3"

Fabric glue to stabilize design on garment before sewing

Ideas

• Use a plain classic jacket with coordinating fabric colors
• Include more buttons, beads or rhinestones for a "bling" look
• Use unusual fabrics for back ground designs

Please refer to page 45 for pattern pieces.

Instructions

❶ Cut fan shape pattern pieces from floral fabric. Using invisible or matching thread, machine appliqué fan shapes in place. Refer to photograph for placement.

❷ Hand stitch lace appliqués in place, per photograph.

❸ Use a double strand of perle cotton and embellish front and back of jacket with a long running stitch. Refer to the photograph for design.

❹ Make 2 extra large yo-yos and 7 small yo-yos from coordinating fabric scraps.

❺ Place yo-yos per photograph and stitch in place.

❻ Embellish yo-yos with buttons and pearl.

Patterns and diagrams

Silk Satchel, page 22
Two pattern pieces shown

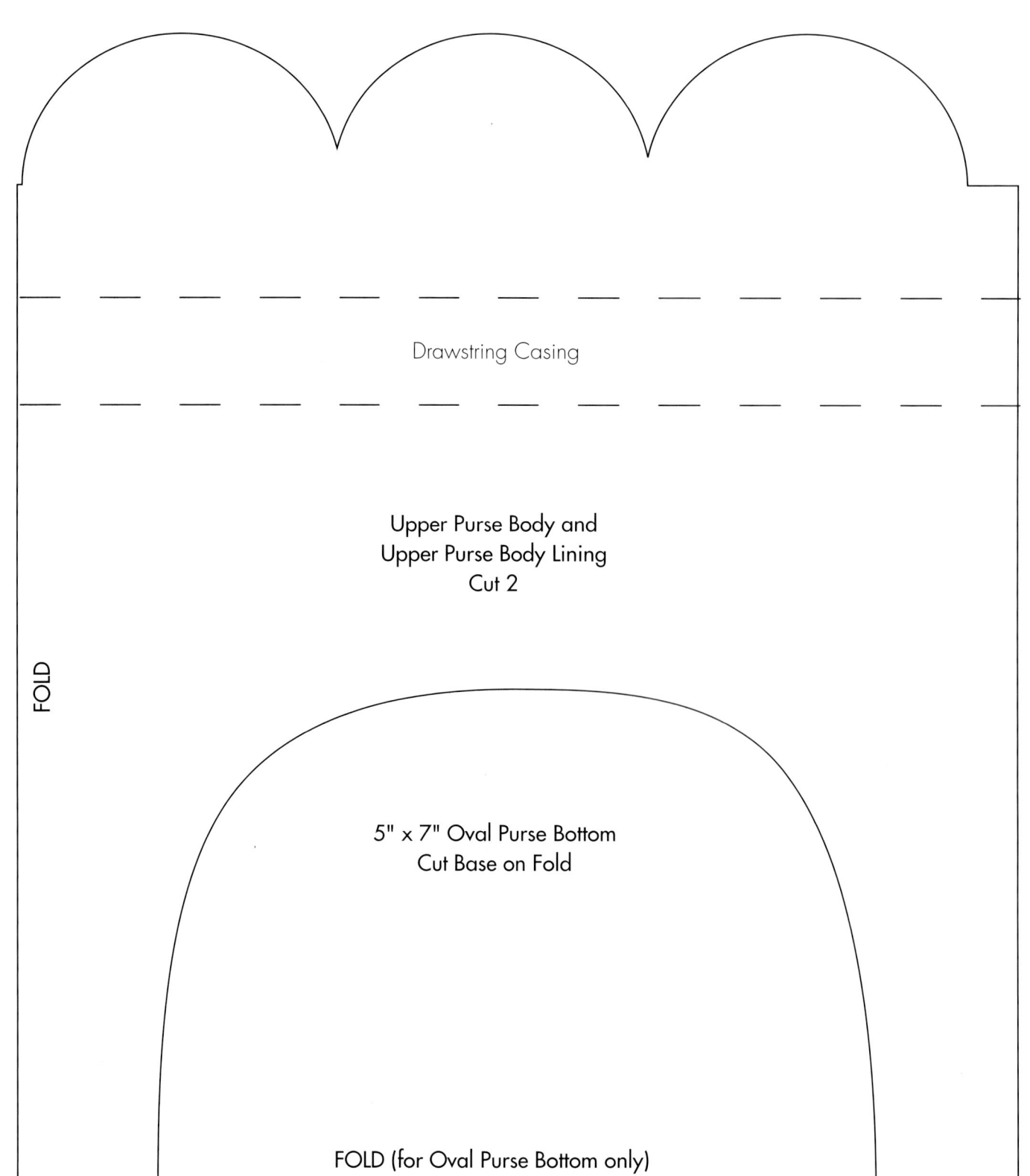

Drawstring Casing

Upper Purse Body and
Upper Purse Body Lining
Cut 2

FOLD

5" x 7" Oval Purse Bottom
Cut Base on Fold

FOLD (for Oval Purse Bottom only)

Fabric Collage Jacket, *page 42*
Three pattern pieces

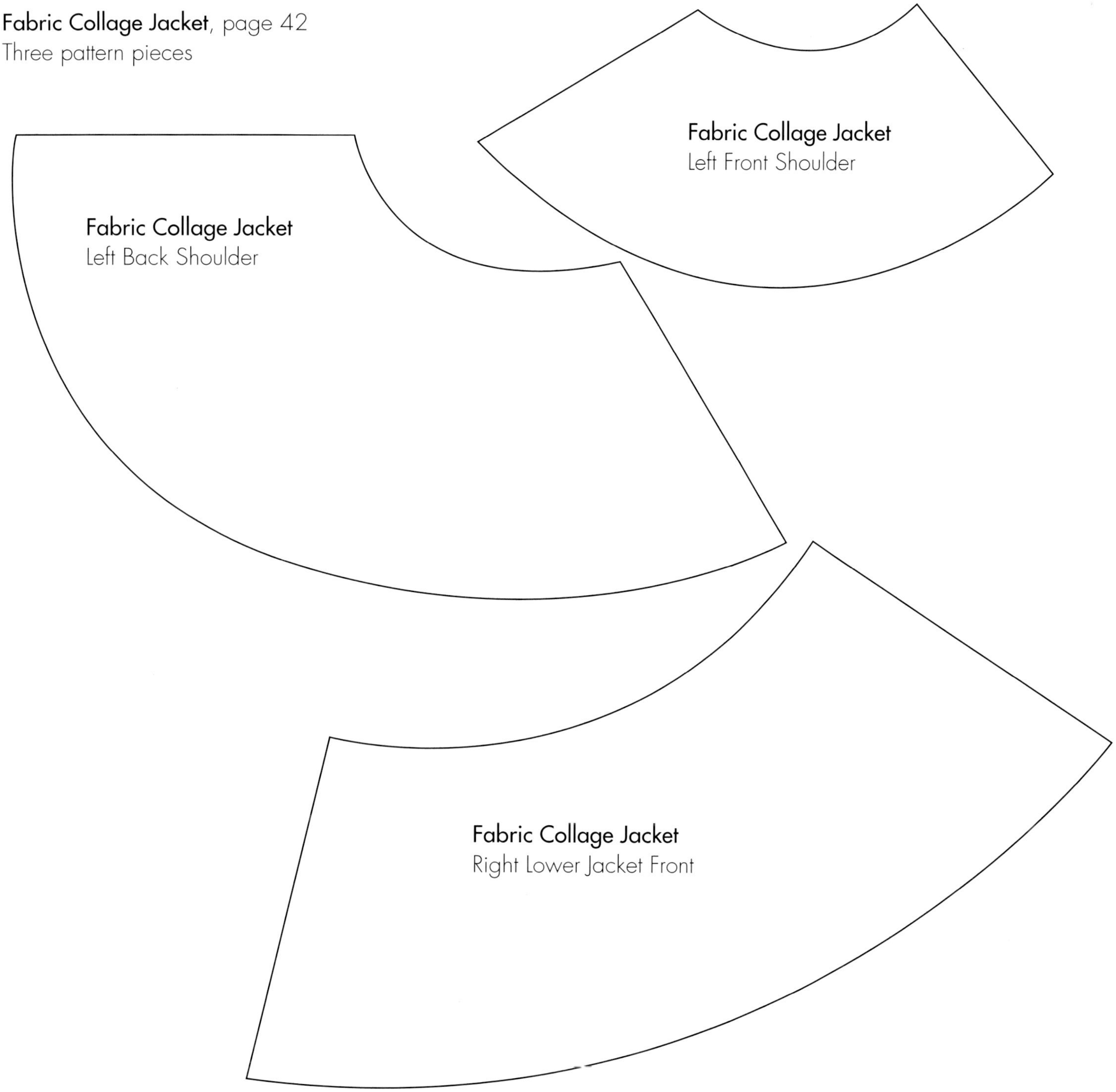

Fabric Collage Jacket
Left Back Shoulder

Fabric Collage Jacket
Left Front Shoulder

Fabric Collage Jacket
Right Lower Jacket Front

Silk Sunflower, *page 25*
Cutting diagram (Full length = 12")

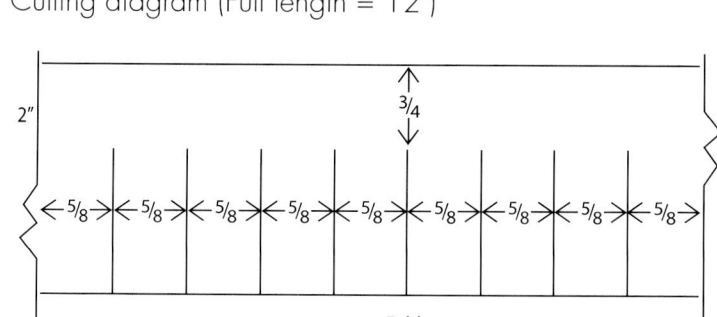

2"

3/4

5/8 5/8 5/8 5/8 5/8 5/8 5/8 5/8 5/8

Fold

Silk Chrysanthemum, *page 26*
Cutting diagram (Full length = 18")

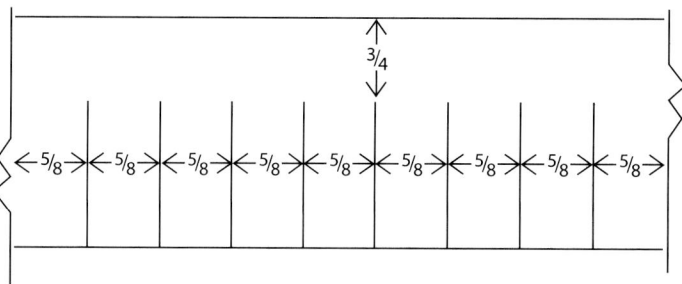

3/4

5/8 5/8 5/8 5/8 5/8 5/8 5/8 5/8 5/8

Savvy Shrug, page 36

Shrug Pattern

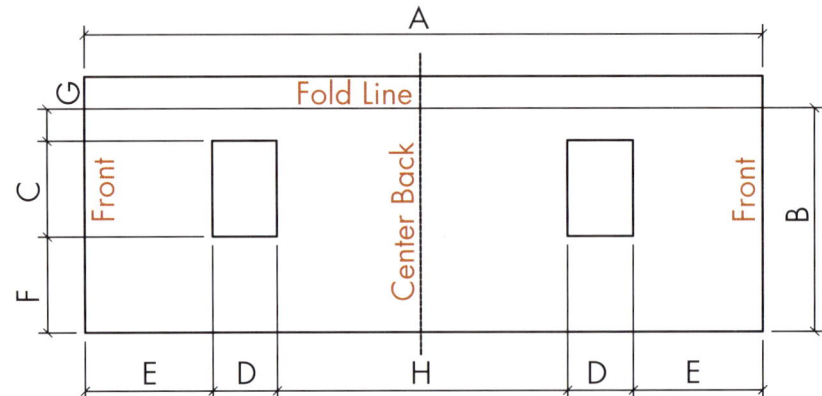

Yo-yo Placement
Diagrams

XSmall/Small Shrug - 156 Large Yo-Yos

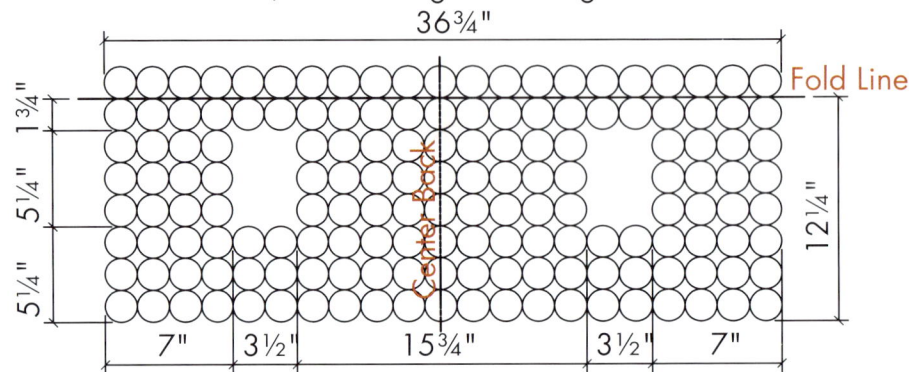

Medium Shrug - 200 Large Yo-Yos

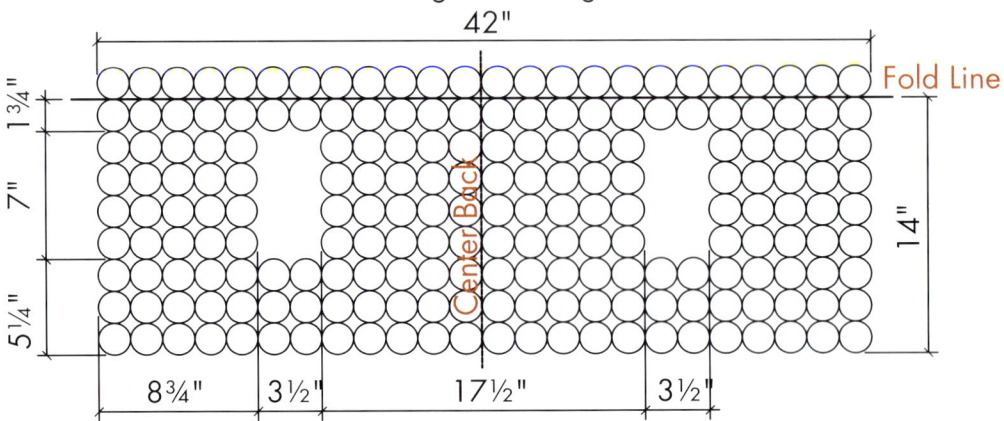

Large/XLarge Shrug - 250 Large Yo-Yos

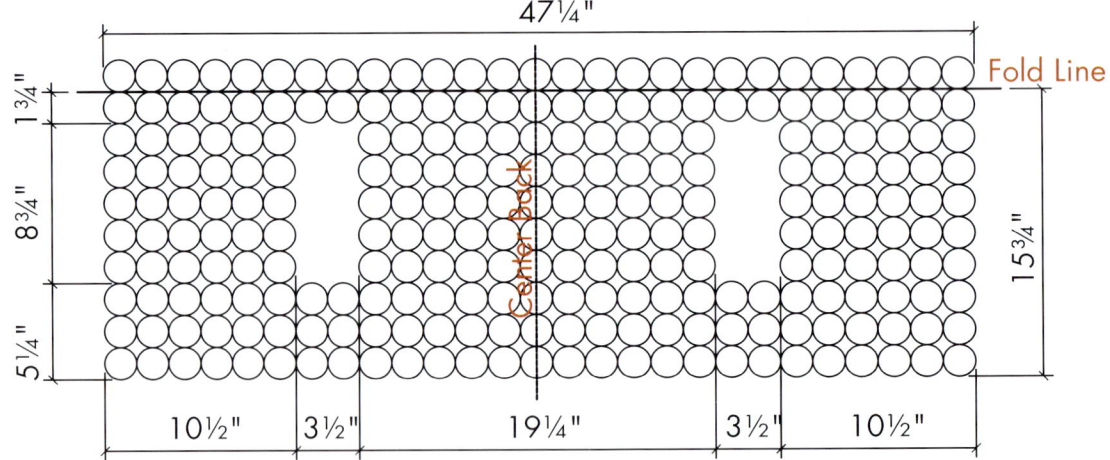